Ciarán Hodgers is an Irish p
is the Sean Dunne National
Pangaea Poetry Slam Cham
Champion. In 2014 he pro
Hours and in 2015 he exhi
4/3 at Amsterdam's NEU NOW festival.

Having cut his teeth in Cheshire, Manchester and Salford, he's performed at Guy Garvey's Meltdown Festival in the Southbank Centre, Lingo Festival Dublin, the London Irish Centre, the John Rylands Library, Threshold Festival, FLARE Festival and in the Royal Albert Hall at the Hammer & Tongue National Slam Final.

This is his first full collection of poetry.

www.ciaranhodgers.com

Cosmocartography

Ciarán Hodgers

Burning Eye

BurningEyeBooks
Never Knowingly
Mainstream

This edition published by Burning Eye Books 2018

www.burningeye.co.uk

@burningeyebooks

Burning Eye Books
15 West Hill, Portishead, BS20 6LG

ISBN 978-1-911570-53-0

Printed & bound by ImprintDigital.com, UK

For Michael and Anne
Reunited at last

CONTENTS

A G A P E

E R O S

PHILAUTIA

PRAGMA

Cosmocartography

FOREWORD

Writing a foreword is a daunting task. Someone cares about your opinion enough to ask you to do it, and you want to do it justice. At the same time you don't want to oversell it, to raise expectations so high that they can't possibly be met.

Ciarán Hodgers is to spoken word as *Citizen Kane* is to film.

Bear with me...

I first met Ciarán at a poetry slam in Warrington roughly four years ago. Now, as anyone who is familiar with slams will know, the silly thing about competitive poetry is that the right person rarely wins. This was no exception. However, at the end of the night we all made a beeline for the young Irish lad who blew us away but went out in the first round, because we had to hear more. There are different types of winning.

The thing with slam is its immediacy; the judges have very little time to ponder nuance, and so it is the flashy summer blockbusters, the issue-based Oscar-bait and the raucous comedies that that tend to catch the eye. They are all very good indeed and revisited with glee, but are never quite as good as when you first saw them.

Hodgers' poetry doesn't just reward repeat visits. It moves in with you, makes a nice pot of tea and lets it brew.

Enjoy.

Kieren King

INTRODUCTION

My Granda Hodgers, who passed away one year before the launch of this book, was obsessed with space. The Space Race and moon landings were, to him, the unimaginably futuristic happening before his eyes. I remember this strange, science-fiction looking contraption (a telescope) in his front room that we were not to touch or even look at lest we move the view off-course.

I was interested in the universe, sure, but in a different way: in mythology, science fiction and mysticism. I wouldn't understand my grandfather's fascination until I had the opportunity to collaborate with Dr Jonathan Pritchard from Imperial College London. This was a commission which asked me to write about his research into the Cosmic Dawn: the couple of billion years between the Big Bang and the first star, so, you know, easy breezy stuff really. Once I wrapped my head around the dense research I fell deeply in love with how the narrative behind it seemed to lend itself so easily to a poetic expression. The poem I created has become a thematic image for the broader work collected here.

Cosmocartography as a word doesn't, in the strictest terms, exist. It's an amalgam of cosmo ('relating to the world or universe') and cartography ('the science or practice of drawing maps'), arising from the idea that constellations can be understood as maps of meaning. We drape stories over them not just to make them memorable and therefore useful for navigation, but also to explain ourselves, the world around us, where we come from and how we might choose to live our lives.

Then, we have our own constellations and our individual stars reflect how different parts of us tell different stories. The brightest, largest stars are the things most important to us, shining like a framework of general human identity. Our personalities develop through a seemingly endless array of new experiences, and softer, more delicate stars appear as we react and learn from our journey. The result is a unique pattern, a map of who we are.

Like constellations, these poems are grouped together. They're collected into chapters named after six versions of love you might find in Ancient Greek society.

These loves are the bright, unwavering points of my own map, the things that are important to me, fixed in place by their rooted connections and anchored relationships, forming the structural integrity of my constellation. In order of appearance they are *storge*, *philia*, *agape*, *eros*, *philautia* and *pragma*.

Storge collects work on family and home. It details the sometimes tricky and tense relationship I have as an emigrant and how where I've come from and where I am are in a constant custody dispute over my identity.

Philia brings together friends new and old. It explores the nostalgia of youth and the bitterness of maturity. The opening poem is an extended in-joke looking back on some of those stories and offering a space to remember a shared youth.

Agape houses work that speaks on nature and the universe. Nature is something that I've taken for granted growing up in Ireland and is something I find myself being drawn to again and again for peace and inspiration.

Eros is probably the most recognisable version of love in this collection. The joyful and painful nature of traditional relationships and sex are explored here.

Philautia struggles for balance between narcissism and self-care, selfishness and self-awareness. This tension came to the forefront as I started performing and working as an artist. These poems are mostly from when I first started performing. Their common trait is a naïve rebelliousness and brashness, reflecting how life was at the time, how not everything important has to be refined.

Pragma is more traditionally understood as the love between, say, an old couple who've been together decades. It's a comfortable, historic love that comes with time, a sense of *pragmatism*. I feel this relates to the idiosyncratic bonds between those who think the same or see the world in a certain way: a love of how things are done – comrades, solidarity. The work here explores the wonderful and woeful ways in which we engage with each other as broader communities and people.

Looking at these poems and thinking about the experiences that have informed them, it might be ambitious, naïve and self-important to think that these poems could speak to someone besides myself, but I hope they do. I hope they can speak when you need them to, and perhaps when you weren't expecting them to.

Ciarán Hodgers
between Liverpool and Drogheda
Spring 2018

STORGE

'The immigrant's heart marches to the beat of two quite different drums, one from the old homeland and the other from the new. The immigrant has to bridge these two worlds, living comfortably in the new and bringing the best of his or her ancient identity and heritage to bear on life in an adopted homeland.'

Mary McAleese

'Perhaps home is not a place but simply an irrevocable condition.'

James Baldwin, *Giovanni's Room*

DROGHEDA

I enjoy hearing English people pronounce you.
Their stiff upper lips tread awkwardly around your rough edges
but you are all soft inside, not that you'd ever admit it.
Rolling like a river out of my mouth,
reminding me of a bitter exit
ripened by the aftertaste of difficult decisions.

We don't always get on, do we?
Sometimes you're the unhurried ghost
whose rapping on the door of dormant distance
echoes into dreams whispering me awake,
but mostly you're a foggy kitchen window,
dishes patient for morning,
a TV playing to empty seats in the one room
because we are together in the other.

You are Saint Anthony pleas,
a sense of forgetting something more valuable than keys,
of misplacing the messy Ordnance Survey of jigsaw memory
because you are wholly independent
of how I piece you together.
The portrait of your landscape is incomplete
without all the perspectives,
but hey, beauty and beholder and all that.

Middle child of Ireland,
the fecklessness of your spirit is a low-budget TV drama.
Yes, that one.

You reserve all the rights to take the piss out of yourself,
and, like me,
you are trying to discover who gave you the stars,
who showed you the moon.

HOW TO BE AN IRISH EMIGRANT

Be born in Ireland.
Leave.

Not for England,
for the love of God, they'll only claim you as their own.
Go somewhere different enough like
Canada, Australia, Thailand
or Mars if you have to.

That said,
if the far side of town isn't far or exotic enough,
what's your problem?

Come home, often.

Suddenly be really into trad music,
Dublin slang and tourism adverts.
Smile at familiar flags but
be sceptical of those hanging outside pubs.
Pronounce *three* and *tree* differently,
otherwise expect the number nine
when you ask for a small forest.

Avoid London. It will feel too much like home.

Discover Victorianism,
how many names there can actually be for a bread roll,
and Boxing Day. Don't ever call it Boxing Day.

Get used to people wishing they could visit
and if they do, roll out the vinyl tablecloth and feast
on chicken fillet rolls, red lemonade,
Tayto crisp sandwiches and a real pint of Guinness,
which, yes, is obviously better at home.
Arm yourself with this fact to brighten awkward taxi rides
and new colleagues.

Call it *home* and *home home,*
discover the word is a wide stance across separate shores.

When you are called *not really foreign*
it will feel like a swift kick in the ocean
but it has nothing to do with rotting roots
and all to do with history books buried behind British teeth.

Remind them you are extrinsic
by reeling off pidgin phrases in your second tongue
risen from dusty classrooms like they were lyric.
Sing *póg mo thóin* and call it poetry.

Support the NHS.

Learn the difference between the British Isles
and the United Kingdom.
Know the fractured histories
so you can stand your ground
regardless of who it belongs to.

Don't ever compare the Irish slave trade to any other,
and challenge those who do.
Remind them of clinging to American steeples
while black bodies burned,
that the oppressed are masters of tradition.

Remember coffin ships when you see dinghies,
how borders are as manmade as terror and kindness.
Know the history of your privilege sits between
sovereignty and the exiled, let it be turf for warmth.

Call your mother more.

Know that *mate* is meant to sound endearing.

Shut up and listen; it would be a shame to come this far
and learn nothing.

Work like a fucking Paddy.
Don't ever allow yourself to be called Paddy, or Mick, or drunk
unless you are.

Pack old myth and solstices wherever you go;
you never know where you might need them.

Just tell people you're from Dublin.

Be proud but progressive, remember but relinquish,
commemorate but transgress.

Spill the parting glass once for the land,
once for present company
and once for the road ahead.

Let go. Your heritage is not a competition;
it is the co-captain of a loyal but untrained crew.

Reconcile how change strikes abruptly now
instead of incremental
with home's objective permanence.

Open your heart to whichever surrogate city will have you,
but, most importantly,
loosen your grip.

Leaving doesn't have to be a knife.

FOREIGNER

A youth trapping sunshine in tombs for sport
became neither the poet under a hill
nor the saint's head in a glass box,
        just a riverbank of bees, a jumping bridge
        and the silent house.

Found my tongue was covered in too much moss
to pronounce the pseudonym I gave myself,
        held too many ember snaps in my voice
        so all the money just burned.

Shouting my foreignness from the rooftops of someone else's city
showed me there was a queue
        where many mouths tasted their accents change
        as *help* became their first word in this language.

By now they know the postcodes
and wear the collars turned up like they do.
I am playing catch-up,
        hunched, tense, ready
        as my starter pistol is recycled to a rapper's tooth.

Golden, and singing holy fire at dawn
turns to wolf-whistling by CCTV poles come noon.
        He circumnavigates himself by comparing
        the dance-floor dust with ashes from his tired wallet
        only to dump cremations in the cup of who minds it least.

Waking to the biting air of a new week,
this new poet on his new hill
rolls a fuzzy tongue around his mouth,
        watches a kid shaking a can of spray paint,
        drumming a gold tooth off the coloured tin inside.

He scrawls *help* under the jumping bridges,
on the empty riverbanks
and astride abandoned homes.

It doesn't matter the language this time
because if we're honest with ourselves,
we all know what it means
and how it feels
to build monuments from hand-me-downs.

EXILE

The destination falls overboard,
still breathing.
There goes another one.

How typical to stay and suffer.
Make, do settles for making do.
To stay is to drown,
buoyant on gesture,
yet the state's goodwill is
there never was a boat.

Learn how mutually exclusive
to support and deport are.
Go now, we thought we heard.
just go.

Home is relearning arithmetic,
quick linguistics, slick new Sabbaths
and when speaking the name of your old land
spits dust and rubble instead.

SIBLING CITY

C'mere till I kiss ya,
and let you slip me a tenner and some fags under the table,
you auld matriarch,
stitched down the middle
with hope, history and heart,
never undone,
not even with all the little wars and woes waging on inside you
and you lacking the money for thread.

You sit patiently and alone in the kitchen,
kettle steam and cigarettes for smoke signals,
signs of life welcoming fresh footprints of new neighbours,
and remembering how each leaving was a happy, hopeful grief.

You speak in negative spaces, absences;
in dirty bricks, churches like top-down convertibles,
statues pulled from pedestals
and unfinished apartment blocks.

You are a Bold Street Bardot, wearing hair rollers on the 86,
96, and an airport no bigger than a Tesco Extra,
companion cathedrals, applause at funerals,
the Cavern in spite of the Cavern,
sunny students smoking Smithdown spliffs
and the pillar of salt we pinch for the lime;
a thousand ghosts traipsing past pier head
where now pianos twinkle,
a girl waiting for her leave plays for tourists waiting to leave.

Lamb dressed as mutton,
mutton dressed in whatever it was lambs wore back in the day,
tipping your taxi men, no-bullshit bus drivers, eye contact,
how no one really cares where you're from
even if it's Manchester or across the water,
street cred rolling rough, another round, another song,
from where we go to where we're from,
but neither more important than if we belong.

CUT FOREST, SEE TREES

Seeing you here
is like being locked in a room
with a stranger's holiday photos.
Forced into chitchat flowcharts of expectant courtesy,
the unnatural rattle of a different accent
slips surprisingly from my tongue,
sits between us like piss in your cornflakes.

Your instinct is to touch everything
with a kind of over-familiarity,
bragging rights for those who never left;
an intrusive embrace whose undertones
barter my gaps in photographs for a boarding pass,
but my mouth is not a marketplace,
more a museum.

I want to talk about how
the world is smaller than we give it credit for,
how patterns of belonging swaddle us,
but my crooked lilt
has crowbarred itself between any common ground,
its choreography is the same as yours
but the music isn't the same
and we're not different genres,
just covers of familiar songs
trying to find out if the original was better left untouched.

Either way, the rivers you know so well
curl just the same as my midnight motorways,
both pulse like golden varicose veins
and passing pedestrians, slick as locomotion,
erode our shoulders when we pause
to contemplate the tops of each other's buildings,
both statues carved differently by the engines of each city;
the steady machinery of mankind mimics itself anywhere it goes.

Else, maybe you're right

and this is a metaphor I've the lost the run of,
a dance I've lost the steps to.

Either way,
my blood has learned well the leaving,
knows travelling is a homesickness for new earth,

so let us both be mindful of how dirt has no loyalties,
we all end under it
no matter how we kick or gather the dust.

We bring abreast our cultural circumference
whose inflexible edges are oak tree anniversaries
but we won't view these woods any different
until we cut the forest
and see the trees.

CALPOL BOTTLES & HOLY WATER

Teabags have piled up near the sink
and Granny's hiked buns down from the corner press.
Not the *cupboard*, the *press*.

Outside nephew cries digging for thorns
and cousin wears 5am under his eyes
like purpled half-moons.

I love this rhythm;
this calm, collected culture
knows itself,
needs no bravado to prove anything,
but sometimes I feel
like the metronome's being swung by a different hand.

I want to push my fingers through the TV test cards,
frustrated at this sterile misremembering
when the truth of our atrophied tongues
is how our history bled
stitching language fixed in its mouth
only to be cut at the neck instead.

I've been looking for a sticking point
but culture has no reflection.
Home is a headspace,
a place with the best Guinness and the worst weather,
battered sausage for overpriced hipster street food,
night-bus punters trying not to piss themselves,
getting the shift, the fear, the sack and the boat,
your wan, yer man, that wagon and the whatdjyamacallit,
a beach breeze strong enough to just batter the blues from you.
Good Friday house parties and Blessings of the Graves,
6am inflight meal deals, trumpets when the plane lands,
Toy Show geansais, new pyjamas
and sweeping New Year through the house.
It's collectively, as a country,
dealing with Bono.

Identity collects like souvenirs:
snow globes, Liverpool appointments, fridge magnets,
summers down under, postcards,
East Asia gap years, keychains, a London internship.

We build ourselves on the lives of the leaving,
but none of it pieces together the silent song
that plays in our meeting,
a harmony of braille tongues whose choir
flirts with chords that would unspool our souls into crying
if you found it.

And maybe we do sometimes,
humming idly in our daydreaming blood,
it slips out like 4am queer theory debates
with Oscar Wilde and Panti Bliss,
like Joe Caslin's murals on every stamp,
how Blindboy's the closest thing we have to a spiritual leader,
like Varadkar because sure, feck policy, isn't it about time,
like MacDonagh slamming body politics in Workman's,
or Markievicz wielding a mic with letters I believe in.
No RTÉ or BBC, she'd say something wicked and real
like *If you can amend it eight times you can do it once more*,
and sure didn't you, filled then with such raw momentum,
thundering across boards Gregory laid for us to break.

Let us dissect the private sector from our health care.
Let us find justice for criminals in suits.
Let us liberate church from state.
Let us fight as fiercely in the North as we did for ourselves.
Let us be ready to listen, to remember all of us who left
when it's our time to receive better than we were given.

We are the twee cliché of faery forts, infallible fish
served with chips on our shoulders the size of six counties,
holy water in old Calpol bottles
like a metaphor for religion as a rotting medicine

would even need to be written,
the eye rolls, the tuts, the notions of the poems,
Blarney stone banter to avoid how we're feeling,
two-pint polemics of how this match was fixed from kick-off,
how their game is distraction tactics,
so let's not take our eyes off the ball, yeah,
it's our goddamn ball, this is our fucking pitch,
are we literally going to hand them the match?

TABLE TALK

We sit like cardinal winds
stretching genetic wingspan across this atlas,
an altar restless in repetition.
Idly murmurating
today's fair weather forecast.

Here we mix like a sea breeze.
Here we gather to be least unlike each other,
to restock and take stock, check in, check up,
to crawl underneath and hear nothing about anything else,
to be held when we are too weak to hold ourselves.

Our geography is crumbs, watermarks,
emptied pockets and post piling into weeks,
sippy cups, rearranged seats,
lingering wine stems, someone's fags
and conversation passing like clouds.

Return me to returning,
a pendulum,
that same restlessness
but always
exhaling
into home.

SUNDAY BEST

Idle toys wait for tiny eyes
while aunts and cousins kick-start kettles.

Sunbeams drape across the skies.
Your mother sighs as she settles.

Apologies roll from bead along bead,
sorrow makes passing a strange prayer.
Roses gather. Proceed, proceed,
for wilting both is wilting shared.

A burial for a crestfallen baptism,
we wet your head all the same,
floating, waiting to be forgiven,
only mourning when we write your name.

The folded pink and blue crochet
of swaddling clothes goes unworn.

The cot we bought for you is sold away
in Sunday best on Monday morn.

NEW SEEDS

When you die
Mam will plant you as a flower in the garden.
When the earth takes
she forces it to exchange:
gerberas, tulips, roses, lilies.
> Look, see how the soil turns with such ease,
> trading new seeds for old memories.

Now, you are not a man easily imagined as a flower.
A tree, maybe, a mountain. The island.

Chips and stuffing for Christmas dinner,
sombreros in the front room,
Mumbai motorways scratched onto VHS,
and the hot snap of ginger biscuits and sweet tea.

There are sixty-one (and counting)
of us left to remember you,
so imagine how rattled, to see my face in the photo frame.

Me, the practically estranged
heir to this solitary lineage of boys,
men of houses I never really lived in,
so I am awkward to be here,
undeserving to belong and besides,
this bedside is a different precipice for the two of us,
both uncomfortable being seen here,
like this, too much fuss in a funeral,
when we have too many years of catching up to do
and not enough now left to listen.

You might not be a flower
and this is far from delicate language
but you are wilting.

Your brain eager as always to blossom
but the body beckons for bed rest,

blue pills and blissful quiet,
bruising tender petals as IV drips spring rain
scattering purple pollen pox over thin,
waxy, pinked skin.

You will be a rose, I think,
prickly and soft in equal measure
but full of colour regardless,
and I will tell the garden
all the stories I kept to myself,
hopeful for a reply on a kind breeze.

GOING VISITING

We go visiting every Christmas,
the scent of cinnamon spice
cooling behind frosted car windows,
crisp cold air
and the tipple of whiskey and red on my tongue.

The gravel crunches beneath shiny shoes,
the crisp strides echo along hollow aisles,
the doors advertising their tenants.

Not even the caretaker's here today,
but the small gardens are well-kept,
decorated with vases, cards, candles,
toys.

To say we grieve here would be a lie.
We save face, cry elsewhere,
our only gifts the silence,
our only news apologies.

NEPHEW

We make our mothers' chests china cups
waiting to break   every time they blink,
for what if we were to remain gone
when their eyes reopened?
It's just that you shine so well,
we need a little longer to adjust to the light.

So grow slowly but well;
you're to be forest someday, kid,
and strength is patience,
with yourself and others.

Remember roots,
to check the soil from time to time,
but don't be afraid to turn to the sun
and grow.

Challenge yourself to do
and to be,
and be ultimately happy, ultimately safe.
Ultimately you.
Whoever that is,
whoever you want it to be.

PHILIA

'Love is blind; friendship closes its eyes.'

Friedrich Nietzsche

'Friendship is unnecessary, like philosophy, like art... it has no survival value; rather it is one of those things which give value to survival.'

C.S. Lewis

THE REMSIL

an ode to a cash machine

We were well-behaved wasters, goody-two-shoes stoners,
Crouching Tiger Hidden Naggin
at YAMO gigs in Navan's church hall,
moshing to punk Prodigy covers.

The biggest boobs or beard bulk-buying Glen's vodka
for house parties, renovating front rooms into dance floors,
John's on fire in your kitchen, by the way,
and ripping holes in all our finest denim
dancing to enthusiastically
aggressively
g a y choreography.

We hot-boxed exes' bedrooms on absent weekends,
sheds in exam-year summers
and tents nicked from various parents
when we said we were staying over.
We smuggled punctured Coke bottles into school,
beside the police station, down the Abbey,
by the honey factory, on the church steps,
round the school gym and in strangers' houses,
learning seahorses don't make good mixers.

It was Tarot cards and Nag Champa,
selling fourteen years of wisdom to people with dice for hearts,
watching the dawn spill like egg yolk over Tara hills,
learning how to spell *magick*.

We were screaming Placebo lyrics at graduation,
hunting for gays in skinny jeans and lesbians in waistcoats,
bringing home each other's dates,
streaking through Termonfeckin meteor showers
and christening your ma's new floor with two bottles of piss-
    cheap red wine.

It was sticky-floored nightclubs raising us
once we got too old to be grounded,
the promise of a Thursday or a Sunday dance floor,
nineties neon desperate to pretend like it was anywhere other
    than a hotel basement and a car park,
going for a sit-down curry afterwards
because they had a late licence,
or a bag of chips because you couldn't afford any more booze
and who goes for a sit-down curry at four in the morning
    pissed off their head anyway?

Amsterdam, the fork that was part of a set,
over-the-counter roll-ups for breakfast,
the dancing dragon and cherry-bomb smoke walls,
Sophie photographing 'the architecture',
Holly high on the Anne Frank tour
crashing in the sex museum to Victorian fetish photography,
Nicola rapping the entirety of 'Gangsta's Paradise'
and Louise seeing God in a chicken nugget.

Driving to camp in damp, featureless fields,
getting laughed at for bringing candles and essential oils
and my self-righteousness when they proved handy for bugs.
Awake between Eoin talking in his sleep and Gillian snoring,
that guy who was a tree surgeon,
the grave we found in the forest.

Alicante, the Veet incident, the Coco Pops 'accident',
Dances with Wolves for pre-drinks
and going home before any of the foam.

We are walking home on sandy beaches after house parties
like something from a Frank McCourt novel
only to get lost and sober up in a Cormac McCarthy one.

We are the Christmas 'I'm home' text,
I see the moon, the moon sees me,

'What would the little fat boy want?',
Gillian's home-made goods at every occasion,
winding Sophie up, Louise's French exits,
me on a soapbox after half a pint,
Ellie flipping the board game,
making 'Peaches' our anthem,
Nelly Furtado's comeback album,
Eskimo kisses, singing to the Cranberries, Chris Isaac,
whatever trad we can remember the words to
and Arcade Fire to annoy the neighbours.

We are all the talks parents will be having after this poem,
twelve pubs, knowing fine well we'll stay put in the third,
but at some point,
between McPhails and the phone box on Laurence's street,
there's a dim, warm fluorescence,
only visible through one cock-eyed half-pished glance,
as we crawl to the club we've just decided is a good idea.
It beckons us to fumble its clunky buttons,
pleading for a desperate score, never a receipt,
and awkward eye contact with the rest of the queue.

A sacred holy site where, shivering in line,
we pray for one more drink,
crossing fingers there's enough in the account
and the bar's not closing soon.
Let us move to N-Trance
and redraft this with each reminiscence,
every new anecdotal stanza.

Let this be a past we carry with us,
a world to step into when we're done with the real one,
for we are here, in here,
and none of us are that far away after all.

HELLO SEATTLE, THE REMIX

for Eoin

We plucked bald the dog that bit us;
you swapped sufficient sleep for a six-hour drive,
a shitty B&B and the only club open on March 18th.

We filled the car with that 8-bit one-hit wonder that tortured 2009
and you got in shits for not being home for tea,
for being half a day away without mentioning.
It must've seemed so unimportant to you,
the day you brought me to where
I began to crawl out from underneath myself.

Later, in twin beds on opposite sides of the room,
I told you I loved you,
immediately followed by
Oh shit, not like that, I mean...
but you knew what I meant,
just reciprocated, unfettered by explanation.

I slept remembering grey cotton jumpers and Irish class,
how the bull's-eye on my back was contagious
but you, being so close and their aim questionable,
would only ever pluck the darts out in private.

The phrase *chosen family* gets thrown a lot,
and I've never chosen to have a brother,
yet here you are without question,
without qualification.

TEMPERED

for Ruby-Ann

I smelt the bonfire on you
before the wind could carry its scent,
knew you'd known fire before.

Yet you shy-shimmer now like the light embarrasses you,
think yourself just a matchstick,
forgetting your potential for fire.

I say you let the smoke drift from between your teeth.
Your heart is just on fire and this song is the burning;
best to let some breath at it.
See how it softens and cools
once the hearth stirs to candles.
How useful this smouldering shared.

So censer until the walls whisper you,
until you are cumulonimbus
and we build temples without roofs.

Make me an oracle of reddened embers
landing cool, resurrected
to tinder for future melodies.

Whistle the kettle into birdsong,
steam like work-a-day catharsis.
Watch how the water stays warm
when the lid is lifted.

How she flies now,
no longer the kettle-fish,
wings breaststroke free.

This is how we become ourselves,
by breathing limbs into feeling
and knowing that boiling

isn't the same as letting off steam
because you've been hot so long
even the pliable parts are marble.
Tempered. So sigh mudslides,
blink brontide, let biting
leave their molars on the floor.

Dance black-footed,
splutter new life from grey,
because we won't know sadness again.
Only love and life and light
for we are all three if we burn,
gladful and free, burning the sun soft from jealousy.

HOW TO BE STRONG

for Emma
for Sophie

Enough about the benefits of fresh air;
close your curtains this time.
Conjure enough darkness so you can fall apart
in privacy and comfort.

Listen to the unused defences unlatch themselves,
taking new shape scattered on the floor:
the silver armour, the boxing gloves,
a pair of don't-fuck-with-me shoes,
something you inherited,
something you were denied.
Somebody else.

Sift through, differentiate the debris;
find out which is your circus, and which are your monkeys.
Keep only what you can carry and what has value,
real value, like the beauty you hide inside whispers,
the petals growing from your footprints
and the dawn creaking around the horizon of your heart.

Leave the house today.   Come home today.
Leave the house today.   Come home today.
Leave the house today.   Come home today.

Get to know this new shape of you.
Dance your heart and hands across all you choose to carry
and those new hollows given by all you have relinquished.

The rest will follow,
but now – look in the mirror,
see someone who, when elbowed into spider-webbed glass,
cleared their throat,
asked clearly and without shaking,

'Yeah, alright, fair enough, but what happens next?
What have you left to hurt me with?'

MEETING

for Louise

Unable to act like adults
however much we were being asked to,
we wanted spilt milk, temper tantrums
and sent to bed without supper,
but it was all black shoes, finger food
and sitting in the front pew.

Mothers discover the hollowness of hearts in moments like these,
and an apology for the circumstance
would be an anchor crashing through the roof
and we're not sure we want to stay here
in this moment.
At least, not for long.

Muffled mute and moored in original sadness,
above our heads
a courtesy wave signalled like lighthouses blinking
across a dark, deep sea,
seen as drowning as it always does.

They knew we'd sort the rest
if they just got one of us
safe to shore.

STATUS

for J.A.

Is all this neon what they meant by there being a light?

A glare blurring the shadows around your features
leaving a likeness that tries to reconcile two opposing ideas.
You died.
You didn't.

Homage beholds and bleats,
pained less by numbers,
but I can't help thinking that in my awkward, distanced view
underneath all grief snores the beauty of life waiting to wake,
the truth that there is kindness in forgetting,
not that I or any of us want to,
we're just toying with the thought of being let up for air.

Instead we sink
holding heavy memory machines,
only able to touch screens.
Comfort stops at surface tension and
our poorly plumbed hearts flood
until there is nothing to do but pour over,
dampening old texts, emails, messages, photos, videos.
All drought-ridden rust and inert memorabilia
made of permanence and performance.

You'll be edited into hagiography, obviously,
regardless of how little any of us are saints.
You found more genuinely precious things in messiness,
which I would more than likely object to,
no matter my stance, because that's what we were like,
presented like opponents to each other.
I've since wondered why we felt such a need
to prove something to the other.

Respect, perhaps, I'd like to think,
letting a little gold cling to your edges now,

despite how little we understood of each other, of ourselves.
Were we really young enough
to think we could improve each other?

It bitters me that you are all past tense
and that this can only be present,
filtered by thinking maybe we weren't very good to each other,
in the sense of being unable to really listen,
but we were friends, whatever that might mean.

As public sorrow floats to you like an unstoppered basin
I prefer to make my peace in private,
if that's all the same to you,
if it's all the same to us.

You might understand why, I hope,
and, from whatever perch you peer from,
smile, content, resolved and painless,
surprised there was so much here for you after all.

DISCUSSING YOUR FLAWS
AT YOUR FUNERAL

for Kashka

You

peeled this eggshell I'd been tiptoeing in,
calling it skin,
like a familiar name
would make it feel less alien.

Knew better than to ask for permission.

Broke me like a fever,
red, loud,
rejoicing at the mess of it.

I
believe energy is never destroyed,
only translated,
transcribed, transformed.

Will learn to hear you with a different ear,
the most riotous gift
and the confusion of its unwrapping.
It won't let me sit still
and

I
love you for it.

Dreamt

I
wore drag for the first time
at the funeral,
because in a poem

You

asked us to wear fancy dresses.
Hoping we might assume the poetry
as a will and testament,
like there is any difference.

Maybe we're most real
when we're absolutely fucking terrified
and yet maybe this didn't really happen,
not here at least.
Only in some infinitely
different places,
wearing jeans, a T-shirt
and there, across the room,

You:

an elephant,
strong
and until roused
gentle,

but do not go gentle.
Go fiercely and firebrand,
but we pray it was gentle,
and soft
and fearless.

We

dress bright
and

You
were never embarrassed about much
or anything at all,
thought it an insult of perfectly good flaws,

held each of them
like a pet from the shelter,
scared, weak and needing a good home.

So we house them in us,
on, after

You.

A badge, a name
that reads

        I
        knew.

        I
        knew.

        I
        knew

you.

AGAPE

'The universe is under no obligation to make sense to you.'

Neil deGrasse Tyson

'The nitrogen in our DNA, the calcium in our teeth, the iron in our blood, the carbon in our apple pies were made in the interiors of collapsing stars. We are made of starstuff.'

Carl Sagan

COSMOCARTOGRAPHY

> 'Love is born into every human being; it calls back the
> halves of our original nature together; it tries to make one
> out of two and heal the wound of human nature.'
>
> Plato, *The Symposium*

The Big Bang is that guy on derby day
who swaggers onto the pitch,
kicks the ball over the fence
and pisses along the halfway line.

Later, he'll take all the credit
and call himself Man of the Match.
We know he was quite literally
the warm-up act, the national anthem,
a rabbit from a hat.

See, it was how he exploded like a bomb in a sci-fi movie,
how he pushed space and time into existence
rolling fierce and first against the encroaching dark
until, fatigued and cooling, settled subdued
like waves breaking back into the sea.

The taste of potential in the air now,
the right molecules sank to their right places
and our boards were set
but silent as death waiting for footsteps
to resurrect them with purpose,
but, see, life, at this point,
is just a closed circuit.
A city of ships-in-the-night atoms,
bachelors typing rom-coms
with girls next door swiping for nice guys.

They idle around each other,
patient for plot points to disrupt
the status quo of this literal dead air,
these infinite empty stages,

blank pages like you've never seen.

Yet a scene slowly starts;
somewhere indescribably vague
there's movement, a confluence of atoms
and Adam is abruptly introduced to Eve.

Loving tempers their lips tense and tender to touch,
countered only by the heat such touching makes to part them.
> Here I remember how quickly we imagine gravity
> like a person could be the centre of something,
> forgetting fate is a straight line,
> choices swirl into waltzes,
> but our hearts drum blood and iron
so maybe magnetism isn't a wholly inappropriate deduction,
perhaps love is both a homecoming and an introduction.

The ionising lovers hold each other tight,
fusing bodies into a third life,
a first light, inviting infant gods to wake
who just roll over in nebulae beds
waiting for breakfast to be on the table.

Kissing strikes matchstick lips into newborn,
first-breath fireworks. Lights so violent
Guy Fawkes and Walt Disney would've shat themselves,
but, given enough time, the honeymoon heat wanes
and adventure itches for elsewheres.

The majestic trajectory and trauma of birth
set us toward the discovery of new orbits
and that is how the adolescent light found us.
Right time. Right place. Right potential.
It fed our foliage so we might eat,
calcified us so we might stand,
burned us so we might feel again.

So here we are, all grown up and
unable to recall the prologue encrypted in starlight,
their freckled chaos turning to constellations
where we sketch new cosmocartography,
letting north-star instinct grant us the fortune of full-steam home;
where we understand the passing of seasons,
the position of pyramids, heroes, monsters
and the godhead halo that shattered the desert dark
for a caesarean symphony
when Bethlehem bore beauty in a birth.

We will always look up, be it for faith or reason,
but their marathonian distance will continue to dizzy me.
They end reaching us and rotting;
we carry their coffins in the firmament
like jewels in some forgotten crown,
unaware we're both curiously stretching towards the other
like amnesiac ends of the same curling snake,
looking from across the gap between teeth and tail,
an epoch lying between every scale,
so when we lift our eyes
the vertigo of our limited vision sparks us
and wonder immolates us senseless because
all bodies hold fire inside them,
celestial or not.

Just as light outlives its sources,
our twinned loss reaches us translated into awe,
too large and deep to understand,
so we extinguish it by pulling the dark sky down on top of us,
crumbling midnight silence into a rubble blanket,
forgetting light for a time.

Burying to grow warm like a seed,
we become a monument of pain passing
forgotten and unfelt,
resurrected in unlearning
and the hibernating heavy on our chests.

And then the light comes looking,
hunting for shadows it left lying around.
It'll melt your metal resolve to molten mortality,
whispering stories through the soil in rain-trickled rainbows
till the solitary sediment becomes a stained-glass window.

It'll teach you how stars have generations,
how, reincarnated with each dramatic end,
we are all just heirlooms of each other,
perpetual reproductions,
as if loneliness were both a homecoming and an introduction.

Then in the darkest corner of the least likely place
a bright paradox unlocks, illuminating your ribcage.
Peel it back,   ask,
Is this what you're looking for?
Here, take it, I've been keeping it safe.
The way you kept me safe,
brought me home, showed me hope.

You will be ignored,
but, in this gap between speaking and being heard,
flourish.
You sought this journey,
discovered that there is only emptiness,
a void where meaning has ended.

Yet what an apt destination for prayer,
that after all our questions
we would have only silence for judge and counsel,
that nothing would be the exact instruction
and somehow death could be both a homecoming
and an introduction.

SWEEPING STARS

Black as his nail beds,
he scrapes near a thumbful from his empty pockets
and winks, erupting hands to cast nebulous soot about us.
Proud and paternal,
God stands amongst his cosmos of glistening
grey grains which saunter instead of drop.

Slowed by the drama of their flight
into shimmering sunlit zodiac,
a lion roars through the shapes in
this mapped bright midnight.

He asks what's important, and I tell him the stories.
A smirk fishhooks his mouth
and the mythology plunges.
Soon I'll be sweeping stars off the back step;
the lion is dust, dropped and distorted.

Everything falls, even stars,
but once buried change to dirt, trees,
to farms and their roots,
to our work and this rough, black fruit.
It's a happy, homeward thing
and their falling
didn't make thinking they wouldn't
any less magic, now did it?

TIME, LADIES & GENTLEMEN

It is still last night by the time
this bruised mind of mine   .
heals the torn gold from glittered evenings
into a dawn of slow, simmering pink.
Pink as cheap plastic pearls.
Pink as alcopop lips.

I sink between cracks in the street,
melted by a symphony of luggage over concrete,
a cement percussion dragged along by a sweet couple
who are a page fresh for the day to work with,
where I am muddle-drafted and crumpled.
A forgotten receipt striding into the overdraft.
Lecture notes found a week after deadline.

I feel like a fossil, clung to with the dirt of history;
the taste of prologue lingers like cheap spirits and flat mixers.
The night persists, trailing after me like a wedding party
singing 'Foxtrot Uniform Charlie Kilo',
singing 'Chelsea Dagger',
singing 'Sex on Fire'.

The sun, having gone round and returned like a scout,
like a tourist, like a sightseer,
turns and asks me,
What are you still doing here?
I say nothing. I say, *Nothing.*
I say everything.

MORNING MOON

He leaves to paint
the morning a crepuscular shade of *wake-up*,
but he's forgotten
to clean up
after himself.

Her face remains in the eggshell dawn
like a stamp,
a tell-tale ruffle
in sheets that foam like clouds.

Through his haste we know she
sometimes still
stays the night.

LOVE LETTER TO A RED PLANET
FROM A BLUE ONE

You are scarred, a child too near the fireplace,
as if your proximity was, by itself, shameful,
as if this grand flame burns for us all to ignore it.
Perhaps we should condemn the day and grow nocturnal,
for who wants to watch the spark that will end us catch?

As your toes gather flecks of cooling ash
you know how time has its way of romancing spite.
So never mind our turquoise;
it is only brief and cold, slipping through our fingers.

There's little use knowing its depth is the same as any other blue,
so we kiss in the rain to forget we're getting wet,
but all it's taught us is how rust follows every thirst.
So find contentment with your rosy cheeks,
burnt, blistering, boiling as the hearth nears.

You have the glory of being blameless and alone;
it will take too long to turn us to steam,
and by then we will be desperate enough to welcome
whatever fire wants to consume us.

OUROBOROS

These fleshy fractals
    of genesis and wreck
        contain what contains us;
            our generations, the bony effigies,
                gathered in the same snake scurf,
                    where zealots pursue a
                      swelling of the

yield, and
    philosophers venture
        to arrest all eventualities.
            Still, these governing magnets
                move us like ferrofluids
                    through the scaly

hourglass.
    We are futile students
        watching an escaping end.
        What we call eternity,
            in the larger sense of things.

DAISY CHAIN

And so we dance,
tracing tattoos through the air,
elliptical trenches
dug deep in this spinning clump.

Humanity's geometry
                    is a waltz
            with us

dancing on the underside.

We look up, see what watches,
mirrors looking into mirrors
ad infinitum,
a daisy chain of possibility,
                        bracketed
                by what makes us
        shadows.

MAGIK, WITH A K

Crumbling away from my weak-rooted feet,
the soil pulls away like an end-of-show curtain.
Convinced this shrinking stage is just smaller in comparison,
my wilful ignorance is best only by my arrogance.

I remember when the earth made complicated shapes,
when worms taught secrets like a torn and scattered dictionary.
Pieced together it spelled something bright, alive and important
and I can't help feeling that if there was a point,
we've gone and missed it.

NYX

Shocked waking
by the water wolf lashing a soft paw on the window
like it has a thousand heavy feathers for claws.
Behind, knuckled pillars of pearl
untangle slowly against the obsidian sky in
a rip of shock-white paper.

Stillness sits in the air like static
and my mouth is a cloud,
pre-petrichor wet, the spit a soup.

I write in the gap between story and sequence,
all remix and plagiarism,
like I've repeated it so often
all sense of understanding is lost.

The night holds me like rain in a sober well.
Curled in the black cradle of the witch's arm,
sense seems like a stolen thing.
Meaning is a ritual
and the ceremony sometimes stands on us.

EROS

'Such wilt thou be to me, who must,
like th' other foot, obliquely run;
thy firmness makes my circle just,
and makes me end where I begun.'

John Donne, 'A Valediction: Forbidding Mourning'

BLINDSPOTS IN BLOOM

It goes without saying
that I made up the best parts of you,
but what if I made up the worst parts too?

Can a palm really be as violent as a fist?
Could a mouth ever be a slapped wrist?
Is trauma nothing more than a poem?

Do eyes really change from lighthouses, flares,
to will-o'-the-wisp torches and glowing cigarette stares?

The colour of them lingers like a sigh of smoke,
orange sepsis of an aura
sat up in bed like a sated forest fire,
      peaceful after each stolen little death,
      each small murder.
Me slipping into rusted streetlights casting marbled magic
against the second-hand intimacy wafting beneath the curtain.

I crawl up each line of light,
escaping the tinged house creaking in its corners.
Innocence made you shine,
nothing now but a naïve gild,
a rotting reversed, sharing swapped wrong.

You are the question mark in the title
of an earlier draft of this poem,
the curve uncurling to learn
love is not sandpaper,
not the backseat of your car,
not that bitch who takes my message beep after beep,
not lighting one off the other,
not come-down or the opposite of lonely,
not imposition nor imprint,
or defending the rope by kicking away a chair.

So why am I denying the click in my jaw,

the shape of your knuckles, eyewitnesses?
Whose sunflowers are these in my blind spots?

They bloom, stretch and cover cavities of silence,
a cave of insubstantial narrative
that I read like a scholar,
but will the forensics of understanding
feel like forgiveness
and, if so,
who for?

HIM, AND ME

Crumpled limbs find uncomfortable comfort
between us like crisp, damp leaves
closed over in a book that slide in, out of pages
whose words haven't been revised.

      Dangerous things are quiet, subtle grains of sand
      escaping pockets, once checked,
      found empty of the respect
      you put there beforehand.

It must have slipped down a throat in the half-dim night
when he placed it under a tongue with his own,
or else gone by impersonating coyotes
all dressed in lambskin and eyeliner.

      Stolen, as thistle meadow arms stretch
      over the lunar shores on the small of a back,
      learning where it best might lie.
      He dreams of making toothpicks from bedposts,
      meticulously flossing the polish once spent.

Him, and me,
we sleep sad separate dreams
cast from the mould of smooth marble
whose covered moss can be so easily removed.

SOLVENT

I hear a recognisable,
almost copyrighted violence in how well he handles silence
sitting stuttered, shaken and solvent
across the table,
at the end of my lips,
in each other's beds;
      a perverse déjà vu,
      we remember a misplaced similarity,
      we are both where he was not meant to be.

We'd feel hurt if this didn't feel like such a bad idea.

This town is a tapped phone,
a switchboard of tin and string
where hushed wires, desperate to move,
sentence us in Chinese whispers along untrustworthy rope,
betraying a conversation that started before us,
with you repeating his name as if your tongue was on fire
and if you kept talking my shadow would disappear
from underneath where he stood.

We meant to dissolve in each other,
but instead it happens as another collision.
An attempt at kindness failed.
Closure, minus all the context.

WATCHING CLOCKS SMACK THEIR
HEADS AGAINST THEIR CAUSE

And so we leave the future
for another day,
severing like a deathbed,
slow, fond and embracing
but tired too.

Yet kindness lingered
in the hard lick of our last kiss
like sugar in the chalk,
paint on a brick,
mirrors and mist.

Saw a sliver of distance
rolling out like dissent calendars and
all the watches stopped in our sleep.
Their hands rage for each wilting second,
faces smack their heads against the cause.

They crave to break levees, to wash into the next moment
where release would carry us like driftwood,
would reset their faces and let them flow undammed.

At least then we would know what to do
instead of treating flotsam like firm earth,
ignoring the soft and solid uneasiness;
one kick and off goes the give.

Forgot we were bedrock,
that we could carry oceans
if we stopped worrying
about who wasn't holding what,
whose blood was whose.

I see you now in every vein,
each canal,
all water's purpose

and its departure.

Leaving only seagulls in the Saturday evening car park,
pubs in the hazy-gilded morning,
the runway just before landing
where gravity ties your shoelaces,
puts a toe in its mouth and sucks.

A temporary weight, like sinking
and the sudden, imminent

landing.

ON BECOMING AN EMPTY ROOM

What happens to an empty room?
Does it become an altar of semi-loss
opened by blood poured in to loosen the lock?

I think how I would become a crypt,
a cavern of death-air
waiting to know leaves
whispering fresh beneath the door.

I imagine we meet at a birthday
in a bar
years from now,
awkward, estranged.
Asking how you are
feels like opening a box of lying clocks.

You look different,
me, same old, all tired and rushed-seeming.

Parting is a heavy thing.
I have dragged it with me since I saw you last
like a limb I intended to return,
a phantom itch
you've been scratching in your sleep
and I pray me a loss,
that you're wrestling patience in my absence
but your feet traipse like seasons,
breaking me as an unseen dawn.

You seem happy;
each small joy empties me in bucketfuls
of lung-sickened sighs that I carry
careful as a cannonball.

COUNTING MONSTERS

1   Under the bed, shapes of coats in the night,
blinking eyes between blinking blinds
and a mountain of masks mocking my mortality.

2   The constant ticking of honest clocks,
how consistent hands print each moment lost,
how the noise it makes marks out a loss
and counts their dots once the tocks are tossed.

3   My parents crying.

4   You, who I brought home
to unpeel in the kitchen like I owned the place
with eyes like wolves admiring the moon.

5   Bringing poems to a woman who
snapped each neck like she was making soup,
how you laughed.

6   Spirals cut onto cisterns with credit cards
and sleepwalking with bleach and a cloth,
scrubbing peroxide-clean dreams in between those
    dirty tiles.
How the smell was lavender to you.

7   The man in our bed like a crash-test dummy
so you could learn the weak spots,
how the blood gnaws at his own weak clocks now
like an impatient hell.

8   The beast who never showed when I needed him,
not in books, bottles or at my niece's funeral.

9   The river that would've been less painful a lover,
a caress in place of a fist,
your love's a cyst shifted between us in pulses and
the water would only have hit me once.

10   These years since and
      how I will not be there
      when you count these monsters for yourself.

9   Retrospect. Hindsight. How time's
      a friend once its hands have had you familiar.

8   I have set your bundled bones on fire with my tongue,
      because I might know how to love horrible things
      but I'm learning to leave less splinters in my cheeks now.

7   Learning the language of shadows.

6   Dreaming in mathematics.

5   Making a spine a skeleton key.

4   The mundane purpose of this ink alchemy
      because if dirt can be diamonds then I can make do.

3   The lion who opens its jaw not when it is forced.

2   Golden.
      Silence.

1   Those broken necks spent like snapped matches,
      how they will someday learn to be supple
      and bend into the angry wind of cynicism
      to prove how hollow its conviction.

DO YOU REMEMBER LETTING GO?

Feeling knuckles redden from white
like you didn't care about floating or drowning anymore,
how it was this desperate raft
keeping you from either this whole time?

How fingernails dug deep into crumpled palms
like ellipses until the brackets
broke and you bled all the unsaid things
that'd been rolling around inside you
like a rock in the washing machine?

Do you remember the first breath after,
like a fresh flower, a sea breeze,
a perfectly timed and punctuated
fuck   you?

Do you remember the sleep,
the refracted living,
showing you all its simple magic is impossible at day?
Do you remember not caring much for magic,
preferring the unpurchased value of lay difficulty?

Do you think this will be difficult or worth doing?
Do you think he might do it for you?

Do you think he is magic?
Do you think he will resurrect, fresh and unwavering
like the vast desert you've been dreaming of getting lost in?
Do you think you're just dizzy from oxygen, or the lack of it?

Do you think that's his hand over your mouth,
his pinch on your nose?

Do you think maybe all magic is human
and that shattering yourself like stars across a night sky
might make this easier than it needs to be?

ON LOVE

'Nor life I owe nor liberty, for love is lord of all.'

Joseph Campbell, 'My Lagan Love'

Far from patient, really,
more quick with the opportunity.
Not inherently kind either,
but a constant exam of kinks and triggers
which dishonours us all, delighting in the individual evil
of our self-seeking arguments.

The vulnerability of intimacy
forces grudges close to our chests while
poker faces taunt doubt and despair,
siphoning breath from faith,
destroying us in its clumsy infancy
and animating our adolescent senses
into an untrained instinct with no language.

You are a distraction from yourself,
the secret upon which all this is framed.
Anteros. A giving that takes only to give again,
that feeds to be fed,
more than sums;
the family behind and the family in front,
the kingdom where we are human,
have poetry, each other.

This slow flourish between fuse and firework
endures and is enduring
when we meet in endless gunpowder,
the history of all the dust left for us,
them, where you and I meet unparting
without knowing or having to decide,
kept by belonging, alive not by belief
but belief alive by being.

LIE WHERE YOU LAND

When you fall into his eyes
lie where you land
till the snow drowns you.
Bloom into something
you'd want at your bedside,
at your funeral,
on a first date.

On yours
you held them like a snare
waiting for thorns to walk thumbprints
over a petal language
you weren't sure you understood.
You were learning how his mouth was never meant to be
gospel,
none of them were.

Remember
the best forgets the good, so
don't mistake distant rain for your flood.
Weather happens in all ways
everywhere
at once,
you're not getting struck by lightning
just because you can see it crack.

Show him the wallpaper,
that you've waited twenty years
to put your feet up.

Learn how laughter is worth being gullible for
as long as you're not the punchline.

Kiss the scars and marks,
you know them,
they are the palmistry of your two bodies
written together in bed,

let the movements read like the best book,
but first
unfold your arms.
He sees a coffin in your chest
and knows finally
that he wants to be buried.

OLD ROPE

A skyward spine cracks like knuckles,
a glow stick, an ice-cube tray.

A pearl cracks and shatters between two molars.
An elbow's cradle finds the latch behind a knee.
A tongue skips double-Dutch trapezius
till we are unknotted, lethargic and lavender chill.

The voltage in a fingerprint earthed in ecstasy
turns the lifeline of our palms to the pattern of old rope.

Blood allows itself as veins creak open.
Vessels,
like empty houses craving to be lived in
unsure who's the voice and who's the echo,
staring into the eyes of each hollow room
to call its bluff.

BONES OF US

Silver splits our lips.
Impossibly we sit
smiling at the boxes building in the attic,
that unknown consequence of choice.

We wear the grandeur of it and
make other things into relics,
a grand inheritance in spite of itself,
both aged and contemporary,
the silent face and the fact in the mirror.

All gathered in pink and gold,
forgotten and untold
to rise at a later tide
in layers misplaced and
discarded skin separated by seconds.

The bones of us run deep
beyond the glittered reshape,
all flat-faced, empty as a passport,
replaying silver memories
and unwrapping who we are
after all this time.

TOLCARNE

He says goodbye to you
earnestly
like I am not here.
He thinks my landlocked smile will miss you,
but you are a pale, piss-poor puddle.

He says goodbye to you
like a lost love,
the one that got away,
so I make the concession
and welcome you into our bed,
a layer of tides tucked into the edges like sheets.

Now I swap sleeping and swimming,
dreaming and drowning,
but no length of time under that blue roofless sky
takes my breath
like the ocean in his eyes.

LEYLINES

It takes it to rain in Barcelona at night alone
on the wrong shuttle bus to notice droplets catching sparks on
    electrical pylons,
each fizzy snap a discordant orchestra, a misshapen serendipity.

It takes harmony ripe with the pre-empt of dispersion
to think of people as a multiplier of time.
Each second is unique, no?
So why not have time be as finite as each of us experiencing it?

It takes the paradigm to shift, it takes forgetting to learn.
What is a tree? What colour is this?
How do I say *meaning* in your mother tongue?
How do the leylines of grey matter,
folded in coda,
cross and abandon each other?

It takes enough time staring at the moon
to see it as a monument by proxy, a headstone,
a promise, a ring,
as the blue light on a phone with just enough battery left to
    write this,
a force pulling the swell of hearts this way and that.

It takes both of us to make the other now.

PHILAUTIA

'Travel far enough, you meet yourself.'

David Mitchell, *Cloud Atlas*

WRITE SUPERB

Sometimes I feel I should be manifesto-loaded,
should know exactly what to say
and make it really   *fucking*   good,
but in trying to outscream each other
we are all just left silent and
truth's only value is how it's never the same twice over.

> Poetry is a gentle science;
> get the balance right and it's a defiance
> against every hated day and mundane job.

Art demands all of us,
commands compliance between heart,
body and brain as we name the strange.
To rearrange the deranged into something
we can maintain is a skill of the soul

> and we dip ink with quill to
> distil shapes of light called words.
> Bright in the places we never expected
> because the recollected is splendid
> with unsuspected things
> missed the first time round

but found anew
when I put my heart on a desk
and inspect the rest
to see if my lung-cleft is blessed or bereft
once the pulse has left,
once the poet goes.

> Whose controlled hold can make
> bronze words into gold, so let go.
> Send it out,
> see how it comes back changed,
> rearranged into something that's
> exchanged parts of itself with others along the way.

Writing is a maze;
the whole point is to get lost,
to cross yourself on the way back
and not recognise the reflection,

        but for now just kick back.
        Relax, enjoy this aphrodisiac artefact,
        make contact, react and feedback,
        allow the syntax to impact
        and sweep you back when it hits hard and thick.
        I run a tight ship
        so it'll all stay intact though playback,
        you can slow the cardiac.

This is no broken record being spun,
but if you're done and want to quit
let us abbreviate the bullshit
and punctuate the punchlines
as you dissipate into these words.

        Remember:
        dictate, enunciate, sophisticate,
        but don't sacrifice calming our vexation
        singing us back into creation
        because perfection is a scarred and cautious poet
        who retaliates the bored and satiates the curious.

So just masticate rhymes like Skittles,
taste the rainbow every day,
dust the dirt off your notebooks
to write superb,
something great this way comes,
just don't tell me you've not been warned.

DEAR GYM RATS

Dear gym rats, body builders
and health fanatics,

from a poet.

We are the same.

Daily trained in bodily atrocity
for the sake of biology or the apostrophe.
This Zen ferocity increases
our capability for consistency,
so tune to the frequency of this mantra's symphony.

It'll be worth it.
It'll be worth it.
It'll be worthless
if we don't push harder, throw farther,
garner armour to exchange pain for gain because
if this doesn't hurt
we're not doing enough.

Put more time aside to rise and write
in the coffee-warmed housecoat
with the morning smoke,
the word of the day
and the way to say it best.

Gym rats, body builders, health fanatics:
we are the same.

We just use scars differently.
You stretch yourself
to stitch the difference
like magicians,
creating one from zero.

Ours are in the marrow,

hardened over wine stains and rolled cigarettes.
We watch the progress and discuss,
write the process to a synopsis.

Poems profit only when they're honest,
so we sing our instructions, make use of them.
This is how poets are never emotional wrecks,
just monuments.

There's more to life than just exercise or exorcise,
more to body, more to mind
when bleeding hearts fatigued
flood heavy rewriting
silent didactic tactics
from scrawling passive lactic acids
out of a resolve turning flaccid.

Revolution, that old classic asset is just our bad habit,
fuel for higher thinking, so let it sink in
that our cardio is heartache.

We skip silly mistakes over keyboard dictionaries
fighting word play in this phrase ballet,
spitting pepper-spray syllables, lunging lexical brilliance
because the difference in lifting hearts and weights
is that what we hold up doesn't have to come back down.

Our resistance steams from raging lungs
making tongues hurdle the clicks and tricks
of a quick, slick Bic,
slurring word after word.
We're all just absurd nerds overheard bearing our hearts flared,
but
maybe we're not so different after all,
maybe we're both just staring down everything that's ever hurt
and thanking it.

IF I COULD TELL YOU ANYTHING

You won't find yourself in school, but go anyway.
There will be plenty other times to seek infinity in sugar cubes
and you'll regret not having wider ears and
getting only an average grade in teenage rebellion.

When your girlfriend asks you to kiss her, do it quickly.
Watch the shared disappointment make an axis
from where all things started making sense.

Bleeding never changed a damn thing;
you are naïve, a fevered fire scratching itself,
ignorant of the shadows it throws up the wall.

A guide to laughter might help.
There are four kinds:
the genuine, the loaded,
the violent and the misunderstood.
Learn them.

Hold God like a memory,
one you don't mind forgetting
instead of peeling apart clasped hands
to find no clue on how to be normal
having been put between them.

The first time, tell him you don't love him and leave.
The second, that you still don't love him and leave.
The last, well, try kindness.
Let him understand it'll only be anger left when he
excavates himself for evidence of civility.

Listen to the news more, other people more.
Get out there, be the news, be other people;
life grows more livid lived.

Thank your toes for being mighty,
for holding all lineage and future,
and find where you are least liked
and be grateful you are solid enough
to be ignored.

THE POET'S PRAYER

Give me words in ridiculous abundance;
let my ineptitude to care for them
mean they abandon me,
returning years later,
a Samaritan syntax only understood
by the gap between reunions.

Give me growth,
slow and steady like healing,
because every shy foot
is a steady root and
the patient pen dries last.

Give me the wisdom to know when to be silent;
make me an observant thing,
a listened distillation that will touch the tip of tongues
and flourish something recognisable and sweet to swallow.

Give me godly mechanics and a heaven of oxygen,
let me sigh sacrilege between my lips in verse,
let me count the angels dancing on a pinhead
and learn how they move.

SM/ART

Growing up I picked blackberries street-side
to eat while coming home from school.

       Now grown-up, my stained and sticky fingers are
       impossible to lick clean and spell out *QWERTY*.

They once snapped, now double-click through screens
whose blinding gleams crick our necks forward.

       I install Bluetooth in my molars to send you poetry;
       even these beta square eyes need updates

so I can look straight through the solar reflections,
needing protection to see from all this light.

All these bytes come between what's meant to be connecting
the hard disks we slip   into slipped discs, making us

       mute   until we
       dial up, log on, jack in to jack off

and backspace through web pages   .
leaving only traces of cookies behind.

This is a generation of HD, LED and PS3.
DNA? CCTV snapshots and grave-plots POV'd
from the sidelines of Facebook timelines
where *iPod* and *iPad* leave no place for *iSelves*

       so even when *iPhone* around for chit-chat
       I find only tit-tat that no longer sits at
       a table to talk.

Even the severed sofas
stalk the same screens sprouting separate sniggers,
so when I speak, is it at you, or to you?
Is it being liked or listened to?
Are you tweeting or meeting it face-to-face?

And, facing profiles, do you register what it is you see?

    When face recognition is reserved for the lens
    it makes followers of friends and people from taglines,
    those who'll lack that glint in their eyes
    or, smiling, hold every lost opportunity
    hanging in remembered unity
    from our lip corners like invisible mourners,

drooling inky sluice chewed from blackberry juice
that falls, writing itself into a work of art,
becoming integrally, digitally, visually and clinically smart.

AFTER FAILURE

My good friend Failure
wrote to me today and said,

'Pitiful, penniless poet, *please*.
Paint your tongue blue
with enough grape juice and sailor speak
until your fingers uncurl from the wine glass.
Return them to handshakes,
applause, interlock your fingers for lifting.

Let these mudras remind you
how your hands have never been hollow,
that you never needed strangers to translate
any trigonometry in your messy palm.

Sit with your reflection,
see the simmering shame of such similar semblance,
shred crisis into something
you can stitch to your chapped lips.
Taste appeasement instead
when you want a vineyard's worth of pity.

Feel anger itch beneath your teeth.
Let it bite the temple bricks to dust and
bleed your broken molars back into the mortar.
Build yourself into whatever it is you need first,
a fireplace, a church, a gravestone or a stage,
just stop biting your cheeks in the hopes
that your tongue might do something impressive.

Words are no longer swords; they are walking sticks
patient for some future wire where
memories wake like landmines
until we're all barbed and battered from the inside.
No one's making it out alive.
Success is just a mindset, so
free the frogs in your throat with all their tuneless chorus,

carve the air into a cacophony of angels,
write origami memories folding like puzzles;
it will be an unwrapping choreography
of the once-broken mended.

Those
who, when their sanctuaries got chewed into cement mixers,
steeled themselves and refused to be rubble.
So be troublesome,
win some, lose often and brilliantly.
Look how you dazzle,
you just needed the wrong kind of right light,
and all those hands that held you down
polished coal into diamond,
but don't let them change you;
only you can change you.

Stay dusty and rough and dark
because it's from dirt where you started
and to where you will return;
all you can really change
is what they throw on top of you.

Will it be roses or weights, petals or hate?
Did you at least learn?

Did you create?'

PRAGMA

'To build community requires vigilant awareness of the work we must continually do to undermine all the socialization that leads us to behave in ways that perpetuate domination.'

bell hooks, *Teaching Community: A Pedagogy of Hope*

'Unanimous hatred is the greatest medicine for a human community.'

Aeschylus, *Eumenides*

RANSOM

Here is news, unbiased,
all the stories unreported.
Here is paying attention,
keeping up, discernment,
incentive, information.

Here are the heads of state,
ability, policy, transparency, understanding,
education, safety, employment, food.

Here is queer sex and social education
as national curriculum.
How to think, not what.
Innovation, challenge, debate and opinion.

Here, Chechnya as a dogging park,
twinks and leather daddies
spilling enough seed so that when the forest grows
those driven into dirt might be pulled up through thick roots
and breathe free in the fresh sun once more.

Here's a mosque at the World Trade Centre Monument
teaching how violence is bad translation.
Revealing that you can't really trust books,
no matter how much you might love them.

Here is an abortion clinic opened in a Magdalene laundry,
reclaiming choice stolen on the foundations of dead children.

Here is virtue-signalling, being problematic,
clichéd, dogmatic, preaching to the choir,
and the inherent hypocrisy of the author,
of any author, of the concept of author in general.

Here's writing as inane conversation,
unable to answer the questions we ask ourselves.

Here's redistribution, elsewhere equity,
somewhere between a sliding scale.
Here is volume for the vulnerable.

Can you imagine what this looks like?
Can you describe the obstacles and how we'd overcome?
Show me, enlighten me,
drag me into future politics,
offer solutions immediate and strategic.

Have art hold us ransom against indifference,
unlike this poem which wants nothing more of me,
does nothing more with me
or likely anything at all.

BURN AFTER READING

for Sanya

There was a queue for the poetry that night.
We'd smuggled doggy bags of Mexican food
and bottles of house red,
flashed accents like wristbands;
we were storm-chasers
for a front-row microphone splash-zone where lightning,
black as clouds across a sky of eyes, rumbled
and adrenaline raptured our thunderous hearts into applause.

My city whispered across the same sea,
the familiar pilgrimage
struck me impatient like an emigrant,
so I packed a shroud of silence
for a comeback revamped new look
like you'd have to pay me to speak
but instead it's for listening,
waiting to be watered
into an archipelago of bits and bones
from seeds skimmed like stones
till roots grew, set, met and
weakened me into strength.

I wake like flat cider,
digging for cigarettes in dreams of old Saturdays.
I'd forgotten how to burn this curriculum,
remembered only the tornado of two-steps
smashing empties by the bar.

All the books have barcodes now,
even the gentry have been left to homelessness
since pews are not for sleeping,
          so never you mind the length of them
          or how empty.

Mercy's new war
marches like snowploughs for the fallen,
melting to the river named after the life in it,
the wasted, lost and washed ashore.

We are ironic
like Che Guevara T-shirts,
slamming about gentrification
with Starbucks cups hanging off our lips,
moaning holes in socks, holes in pockets,
how pockets are just holes for money to pass through
whilst we're about one Zumba class away
from bankrupting ourselves on privilege.

Show of hands, how many poets do we have in the room?

There's no wine left in Dublin,
not since dawn broke
and the scratch cards revealed American flags
whose 4th of July fireworks bang
and we're burning books like it were the same thing
but the best flint for us is bone.
Bones in the Bataclan,
bones on Turkish shores,
bones in Calais,
bones in Brussels,
bones in nightclubs,
bones to microphones,
so we can just stand there
melting.

Someone's ex suggests pitching tents on stage
so the city sleepers can cook marshmallows
but the chips we've stripped from our shoulders
burn like the memories of kissing in graveyards
illuminating all our grudges as heirlooms.

We never wanted to be witness
but we burn after reading;
this is just smoke.

This is all just smoke
of someone else's fire.

EXIT WOUNDS

Nervous as a bomb disposal
between my flag and yours
I discover mispronunciations
of Canaan, Tchaikovsky, Auschwitz,
Michelangelo, Gaza, Dostoyevsky
like mistaken memories reappropriating me
some sort of pseudo-native.

I think they've been briefed on me in their sleep,
know I've come to swim upstream
instead of against wave machines.
Rats come to learn their mazes and
I'm here to draw its pattern out from my dreams.

We are different kinds of dirt in the same pit.
I lie in certain kinds of truth,
while vice-versà gesture-politic MP MCs
turn policy in poetry slam,
but which of us speaks more carefully?

Words become gunshots, sounding *please, no,*
not every exit has to be a wound,
but they're mistaking maps for scratch cards,
digging for gold with all the gusto their loose change can muster,
leaving lineages gathering like dirt beneath their fingernails.

My fever dreams of internships and tax reports
are wakened by nightmares of how in austerity
they found hundreds of millions of pounds
to prop up the ghost of imperialism
like a Hallowe'en costume made of sticks and bedsheets.

They've convinced themselves diamond amongst coal
and scream down that the weight of change is death.
They'd have the caterpillar
never learn of the wings tucked inside itself,
yet opportunity lingers too much like

guilt in the aftertaste of silver spoons,
so they break bread over bones and borders
forcing shame into communion
and Britain exports erasure again.

I've seen what colonialism can do to a homeland.
It's everything religion taught us
in the hands of those who forgot,
lines us up in pews
marching fingers over hymn books like triggers,
unsure which is more dangerous,
can't tell which they put under our tongues first.

Mine spills with ink-spit,
too much to hold or swallow,
so I write them out.

What else can I do when even this
has become a kind of mourning,
a grief that buys them time,
the grief they were counting on all along?

UNCONFIRMATION

'Confirmation bias, also called confirmatory bias or myside bias, is the tendency to search for, interpret, favour, and recall information in a way that confirms one's pre-existing beliefs or hypotheses.'

Scott Plous, *The Psychology of Judgment and Decision Making*

'Queer is by definition whatever is at odds with the normal, the legitimate, the dominant. There is nothing in particular to which it necessarily refers. It is an identity without an essence. "Queer", then, demarcates not a positivity but a positionality vis-à-vis the normative.'

David Halperin, *Saint Foucault: Towards a Gay Hagiography*

And see there are more of us to be buried,
to be witnessed.
To pass knowingly lost
from temples where silence
is a new and distant grief,
met with clamouring dial tones
like prayer for safe passage.

In other places
news anchors use all the wrong words.
Our grammar is still young, so it seems,
still sulking in corridors,
pulling pigtails and smoking round the gym.

The curriculum typified us,
sharpened the words we chose to
show how self-definition
cuts the tongues that speak it.

This lesson of direction taught us about force,
showed us oppression disguised as dialogue,
desperate for some incendiary distraction

before we found the right words
buried somewhere between headlines,
where ink baptised us in diagnosis.

We might need to burn down our own language
until they stop shoving
semantics down our throats
and mock us for having dirty teeth,
because rather than red tape for gun merchants
we read texts from bathroom stalls,
willing him to crawl inside radio waves and escape,
will them to play possum,
will unwilling suicide before murder.

Rather this *conditional* right to life
than changing a thing named for change.

And all the journalists are talked off sets,
unwilling to stand when they came for our knees,
yet we are the ones that remain unheard
when we are the ones that refuse to be present,
reduced to singular stories, defined again as adults
by panels too busy assuring us we're equal to listen,
too busy reminding us that love wins
to see how hate is killing people.

Feelings aren't bulletproof,
they sour in our chests,
having learnt trauma doesn't give two shits about safe spaces,
how philosophies formed from anecdotes
distract echo chambers with academia
until repeated history is surprisingly unprecedented
and we are much less articulate when we need it most.

Progress is sometimes supposed to be uncomfortable,
but I'm scared our turncoat sentences
are tied to stronger tongues that will speak for us,

define us, name us,
place us in society and apparently obituaries.

So let's unconfirm ourselves and be uncomfortable,
meet their surmounting silence
with a ceaseless, indescribable noise,
let them pass vindicated, wasteless
and the last ones to be defined for us.

THE ANCHOR IN YOUR MOUTH

I hear the word *integration*
like you're pointing to where it touched you on a doll.

That tongue-curving inflection
doesn't need to have made the chain
to know how important the twist.

PROBLEMS WITH PRIDE

'You know, the guys there were so beautiful – they've lost
that wounded look that fags all had ten years ago.'

Allen Ginsberg

i

We've gathered ourselves together in unity
but, see, we've been
lamb staggering around your scripture for far too long
like path-cracks, hand-slaps,
teaching you to abhor this nature of mine.
A chore to question such ageless fiction,
so the ink-inflictions force me
to hide in the tightrope rafters
of the public streets you so reverently master,
where the anonymous mythologies
seize my sin-heavy wedding band
before the strands of my weak hand snap
and scrap society's fabric erratic,
as if the world's apocalypse lay in our meeting lips,
but where his hips hold only me,
there'll be sparks knocking off our knees,
leaving the ground littered with
attempts at our sons and daughters,
until his broken waters flow to deliver,
or she comes in virile flavours
of love.

ii

These parades and half-dressed masquerades
soldier our Trojan crest marching
dispossessed legions of colour
in a rainbow sparring bookended shades against the other.
The banners cry out for freedom
but the people, when you see them,
call for bedpost knocks
and open arms with elbow knots.
We allow pop songs
to right all the wrongs
we can't be bothered to face up to.
It makes this place a zoo
when it's you
and her   and him
and fat and thin and hairy and camp
and dyke and tramp and butch and gay.

We're all but beasts in our own way,
yet all the more the animal when
ignorance cuts like a harpoon thrust,
shame that equality would end with us.

BADGES

'Fighting for the right to get married is like fighting for the right to go to prison.'

Brendan O'Connor, 2014,
on the front page of the *Irish Times*

The adhoc audience sheltering from December's cold nod,
wine-kissed in an almost reverent acknowledgement.
I know better but whisky makes me itch for polemics,
so logic does a dazzling array of top-scoring
Olympic-quality acrobatics.

Assuming nothing, these are friends after all,
but the God's-honest look of accusation
galvanises me against such wrong self-righteousness
deemed friendly fire.

I remind myself
they've never been considered fundamentally flawed
by the law we cling to for a shield at 4am
hoping the crowd is too busy wading chip-bag vinegar
to notice we're paying too much attention
to the pavement to punch back.

They've never switched stations
to hear people who don't understand them
debate how much they'll be given
like a dog they'd rather starve
than resort to feeding it from the table.

To them, Bert and Ernie are just really good friends,
Wilde was just a writer, Turing just a scientist,
Milk just a politician, Johnson a drag queen.

Their history was never the electricity of those who,
understanding this would make us glass,
showed us how to be bulletproof,
how to frighten ourselves into an orchestra

whose wrists creak like lepers' bells;
hips swish, whistling of bricks approaching windows;
giggling the fizzy noise of bottles shattering in the alley.

The requiem that single sigh our body allows itself
when we learn we were unprosecuted criminals
before we were old enough to tie our shoelaces.
The reprisal of even though our hearts are no longer
    accusations,
all we do is damning evidence otherwise.

These petty poetics are spared of proper exposition,
but I'm sure you can remember the conversation
and know it was your name atop this poem at one stage,
but simply, I don't care to explain myself.

I will say, though, that rooted principles are least immune to rust,
which, by the way, is a sickness that eats the host.
Such stagnancy won't spoil my speaking,
my water language
whose mutable countermoves queer the words
unconstitutional and *agenda*
till they read *will you* and *I do* and *yes*
and *yes* and *yes* and *yes*,
till equality feels less to you like grief.

How can we be here to take from you
when you have nothing we need nor want?

How can you be the victim
when it's other people who get screamed at in the street just for
    wearing badges;
the small round flash of it pinned to their jackets,
the word *Yes* met with such spittle and volume?

HABIT

My mother gave me this habit
of blessing myself whenever a siren passed.
God forbid, we are reminded,
it'd be someone you know.

The act seems teased too often in this city,
siren songs screaming down the street,
yet I remained lucky, they passed,
did not stop at my door.

When it happens this is the first thing I think of,
that when Mike Brown's mother heard sirens
it must have been a most familiar sound.

Police are sworn to defend and protect
but I see little threat
in the suspected theft
of missing cigarettes,
with backs turned, hands erect.

Cadets 'forget' under pressure, you see,
so the people
fell to their knees in protest.
This was the most violent thing they could do,
to tempt the lions their share
because history will not be settled in handshakes;
instead arms wave
like they were lambs' blood above the door,
a white flag to mean peace,
but if this is no war,
why then the bodies?

Ever since Roman hands held Bethlehem soil
they have known how to work the land.
They took his crucified effigy,
changed it pale down the centuries
from a racial pedigree that denied him a refugee in retrospect,

carving from the native rood new weaponry,
putting prisons in prayer,
replacing the crucifix for a crosshair.

Cops like that have always pulled triggers on boys like him,
more than once is more than chance,
it's a habit that dies harder than people do.

Change is violent, expensive and unpopular,
but we are allowing the rug to be lifted
and the dirt swept under.

Another siren sounds and I wonder
if his mother
has blessed herself since.

X

in memory of those lost to the 8th
in solidarity with those who repealed it

She knew well before she took any test,
kept seeing equals signs everywhere,
on till receipts, tea leaf patterns, contrails travelling overhead.

Funny, she thought, parallel lines meaning *sum of*
felt more like an X, marking a spot,
a crossroads, a signature, a letter for a name,
meaning *anonymous*, not yet known.

Certainty certainly left lots to be understood,
like the change of her body, Saturday nights,
her morning ritual, fear of the world
and its endless table corners,
but normal adjusts when you give things names,
construct flat-pack furniture,
feel movement, no longer just theory but footprints stretching out.

So what of her, changed a second time,
baptised in a wrong grief, a retrograde death?
There are words for orphan and widow,
but how to be
when there is no word for you?

Made by speechless hands that caress and linger,
we are undone by figurative triggers, by unlifted fingers
and God chose to be a closed palm,
shrinking from strings for puppet movements,
a deus ex machina.
Players count no saviours when the script becomes a deadlock.

Now, I'm not saying we should jump-start shock
any kind doctor's wrist twist in place of
contraception, education or consent,
but when girls need permission to leave

to cleave clean the pink anger men
stuffed into her at fourteen,
she shouldn't need to raise a hand like a child at school.
She was a child at school,
so whose side would her suicide fuel?

In protecting one we've murdered two
and I don't really know about you,
I was never good at numbers,
but someone's not carrying the one
wondrous thing we call law,
which assumes all seeds grow fruit
but, failing, salts their roots behind.

How long had it been since you lined up for mass
when you told her this is a land of Catholics?
Was it pro-life mavericks that put women in laundries?
Was it orthodoxy to put altar boys in therapy?

Don't preach to us heresy; we are broken with it.
Ripped through with respect, a steepled sect salved in death,
debt repaid in the cruel tradition of our unrisen.

It was our love that christened them,
dragged them from us blessed,
and too weak to cry.

We kissed their heads in 'x's as we laid them down,
keep seeing their face
in other children,
at the bottom of empty kettles,
on clouds travelling overhead,
in the silence that swallowed their forgone bawls.
I never realised they made boxes so small.

SISYPHUS LISTENS

The eyes roll in her sockets,
he hears them thundering from the back seats,
they are the sound of Sisyphus discovering another fucking hill,
left after his tongue lifted to speak
        to lecture on freewheeling downhill.

His easing of the road ahead
displaced the earth to a mound elsewhere.
        If there was a name for that dug-up dirt
        it would be properly pronounced
        with an eye-roll and the loud, wet kiss of teeth.

Such is his tongue,
rolling like a red carpet saying,
Here, walk on my back if it'll make you feel any better,
because from where he comes from
solidarity is spelled *m a r t y r.*
        He will need to learn how people are not spellcheck,
        how history isn't an essay
        and that the wisest thing to know
        is that you know nothing,
        nothing at all.

PILGRIMAGE

It was no holy, righteous act,
no immaculate conception.
This was more about touching
than it was about reception.

Chests beat like rapture,
although not.
He was to relic
like she was to genuflect,
to mortify, to cage, to trophy.

Piety replaces patients with protesters,
making propaganda of pain, porn of pregnancy;
open ports tally collateral damage
by how many legs stay shut
only to be prised apart by another man.

These women sing blue birdsong as they go,
a prisoner's imperfect pilgrimage
passing like nuns for new heavens
around the gardens.

RECITATIONS

Were you counting?
100.
     200.
          400.   8.

Did it help you forget their names?
Matthew.
     Mark.
          Luke.   Sean.

Did you give them something to mourn?
Cot death.
     Stillborn.
          Stopped breathing.   Deformed.

Are you still counting
the recitations pawned for penance?
Hail Mary.
     Hail Mary.
          Our Father.   Our Father.

Absolution is a libation for a washed-up body.
It mistook the name for instructions,
repeated until its meaning curved in on itself,
till the dirt sank and made it.
Tuam.
     Tuam.
          Tuam.
               Tuam.

SEX AND THE CITY AND YOU

A jaundiced sun breaks down the cul-de-sac.
It's a beer can for an ashtray kind of morning and,
unravelling the merry mess we made of our weekend,
thoughts drop like pennies from your tongue in a sigh.
Oh my god. I'm such a Samantha.

Casual complacency bubbles like laughter
but I've never heard pleasure
sound quite so much like an apology before.
Stuffed into your mouth
by men who mistake *no* for *convince me*
and suddenly it's not just about this anymore,
something else stirs and aches.

It's Steak and Blowjob Day, Paris runways,
Ernest Hemingway, lingerie, mansplaining, slut shaming,
marriage changing initials, rape whistles, unfair dismissals,
the prefix *intersectional*, ethics based on genitals,
page 3, less female MPs, rhinoplasty,
revenge porn, acid attacks, tampon tax, wage gaps,
abortion rights, juice diets, Pussy Riot, cis privilege
and dance floors like candy stores.

It's war, marching map lines in working-class crimson.
It's prison when single mums can't afford
to keep kids from exploring the streets
because an executive's cheque only affects the perfect
when their sex is male.

It's reciting essay answers like times tables
to snuff the fuse inside ribcages
because right now kids' hearts tick like bombs
warning now or never.

Being schooled clever instead of wise
left us improvising how to run a house,
raise a child or deal with stress

while the walls fall and the cot rots and
muscles knot like pulled elastic snapping free.

Yesterday, I learned the word *phosphene*:
a luminous image produced from pressure on the eyeball
by the finger when the lid is closed.

Persistent light in the absence of light makes
glass ceilings too transparent a metaphor now;
instead it's two fat thumbs like thick arms
drowning pups behind my eyelids,
pushing distant stars into view.

A Cosmos of cover girls
blowing boys and buying beauty,
assuming duty of shepherd, sheep and dog
dictated to them by an industry that knows
how conservation is a fear of what's wild.

It busies you with yardsticks,
stakes to strengthen your spine like you'd wilt,
but they're the same canes that whip rhetoric
and when it comes to it
witch-pyre kindling to play shadow puppets
with the flames they'd make of you.

You roll your eyes now,
think this none of my business,
but I'm not taking the piss.
I've seen silence sink men whose knotted chests
were too heavy to do anything else but drown.
I watch women barb each other
to appear the taller flower
only to be plucked
and die a decoration in some man's hand.

You were born to bloom, beautiful and thorned,
to mean no harm but take no shit.

You don't do apologies,
need no permission, least of all mine.

You are a bundle of nerves and volts,
craving to thunder and crack,
so stop wasting your water
on those who can't dance in the rain.

SHADOW MAGIC

We break the back of language,
zooming in on the personalities of moths;
anxious preciousness goes blurry and lost.

Forgetting unarms,
and your body is a clause whether you know it or not.
Epigenetics chops the tree like the sharp side of lightning,
stealing away all of our stories
by the time it takes for clouds to become mothers.

        If trauma flows forward through time
        then its opposite must go opposite;
        retrospect resurrects.

Inertia kicks kinetics to voice
and a sturdy bark reaches backwards through the tide;
      olive branches arching overboard
      are pithy penance for the past
      but pull the fallen forward,
      ask the ghost its name,
      find one for those who've lost theirs.

Vision heals
coursing pins and needles through phantom limbs revisionism.
Breath is more than a spectre,
frightful and flighty, forced from fantasy;
there is a wider duty in remembering
amnesia like this is intentional.
It shifts the focus in on the fire
when it was those damn moths
that caught our attention in the first place.

Put any broken archaeology you have to use;
weaponise the past,
the ancient and the present passing.
Learn their names, say their stories,
reciting relives the light lost to shadow magic,

because you might find yourself
on the mute end of séance one day
and be grateful someone thought to look back,
that someone wrote your name down,
that you died only twice.

ACKNOWLEDGEMENTS

Who am I kidding, this was never going to be a short list...

First thanks must go to Bridget and Clive at Burning Eye for wanting this work to be out in the world.

To my family, especially Mam, Dad and Anne. I blame yous for all the words in the first place.

To Ben, for your patience, kindness, humour and love.

Special thanks to Mary Kerr at O'Fiaich for refusing my excuses.

To Kieren King for raising the bar.

To Rose Condo, Hannah Davies, Gevi Carver – for your gentle and honest guidance on earlier drafts. Thank you so much.

Louise, Nicola, Ceara, Ellie, Eoin, Gill, Soph, Jay, Holly, Ciara Lord, Ash, Ciara Moore – told you I was going to use that in a poem someday.

Elaine – for your kindness and solidarity.

Maera, Amy, Dom, Brian – for the magick.

Julie, Jo, Angi, Meriel and Robert – for your continuing championing. Thank you.

Jodie – for the space, time and conversation when it was most valuable.

Nathan – I'm forever grateful for your trust.

Seb, Hannah, Dan, Adam, Craig, Tess, Elke – for being ports in a storm.

Sanya and Benedict – for hype when I have none, and London.

Ella Gainsborough – for giving me, and many others, a stage.

To everyone at WoW – for your infectious inspiration.